Bir

Written by Gill Munton
Illustrated by Isobel Bushell

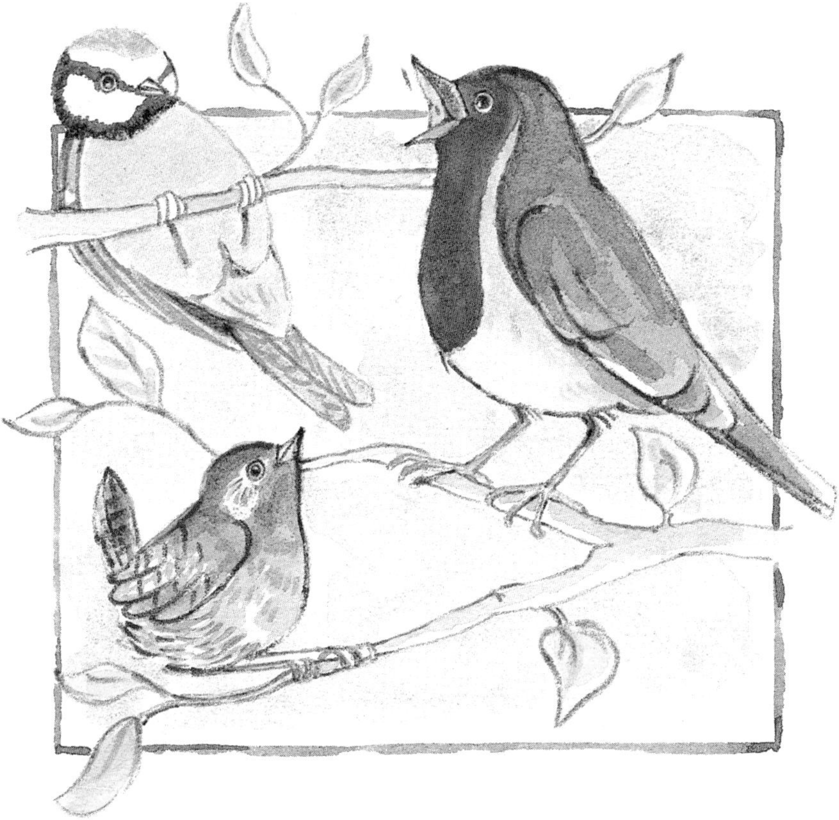

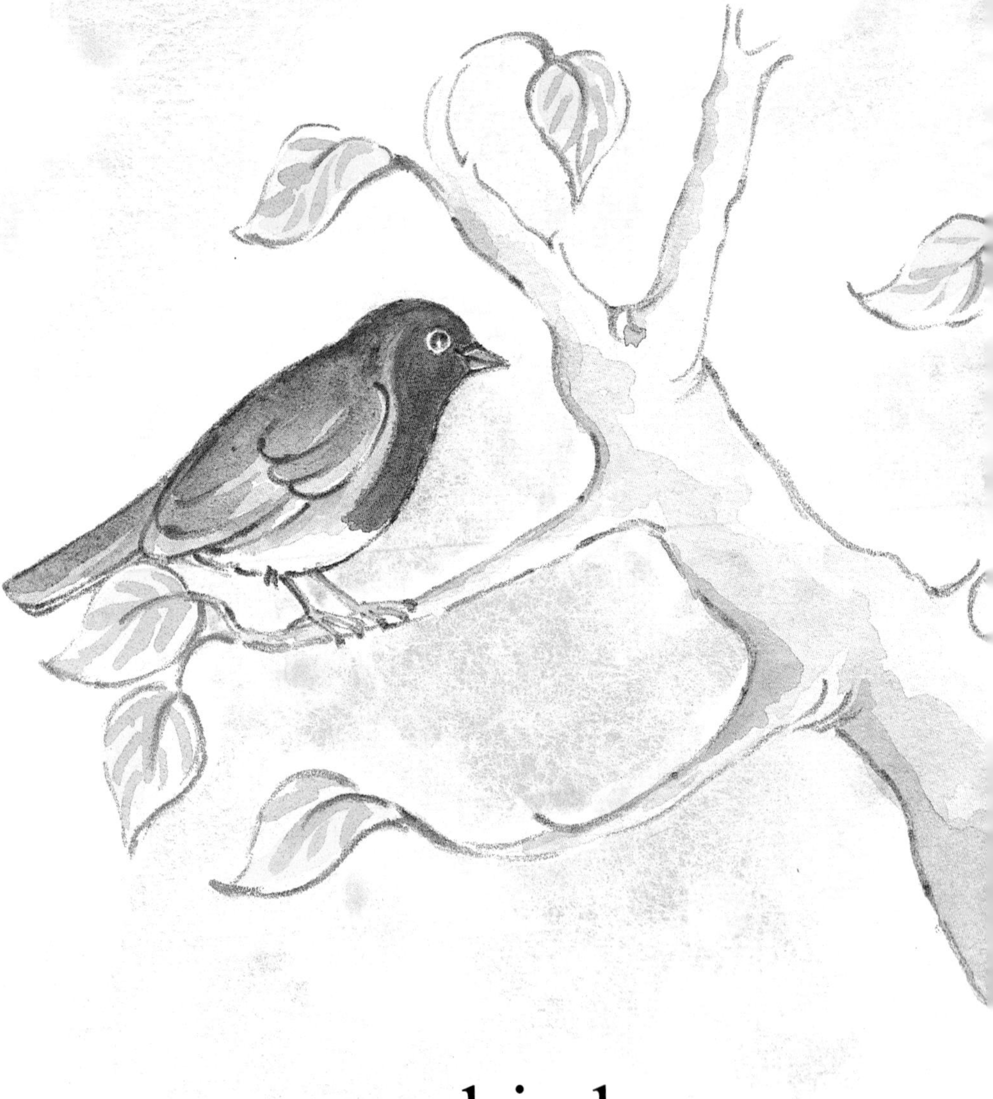

one bird

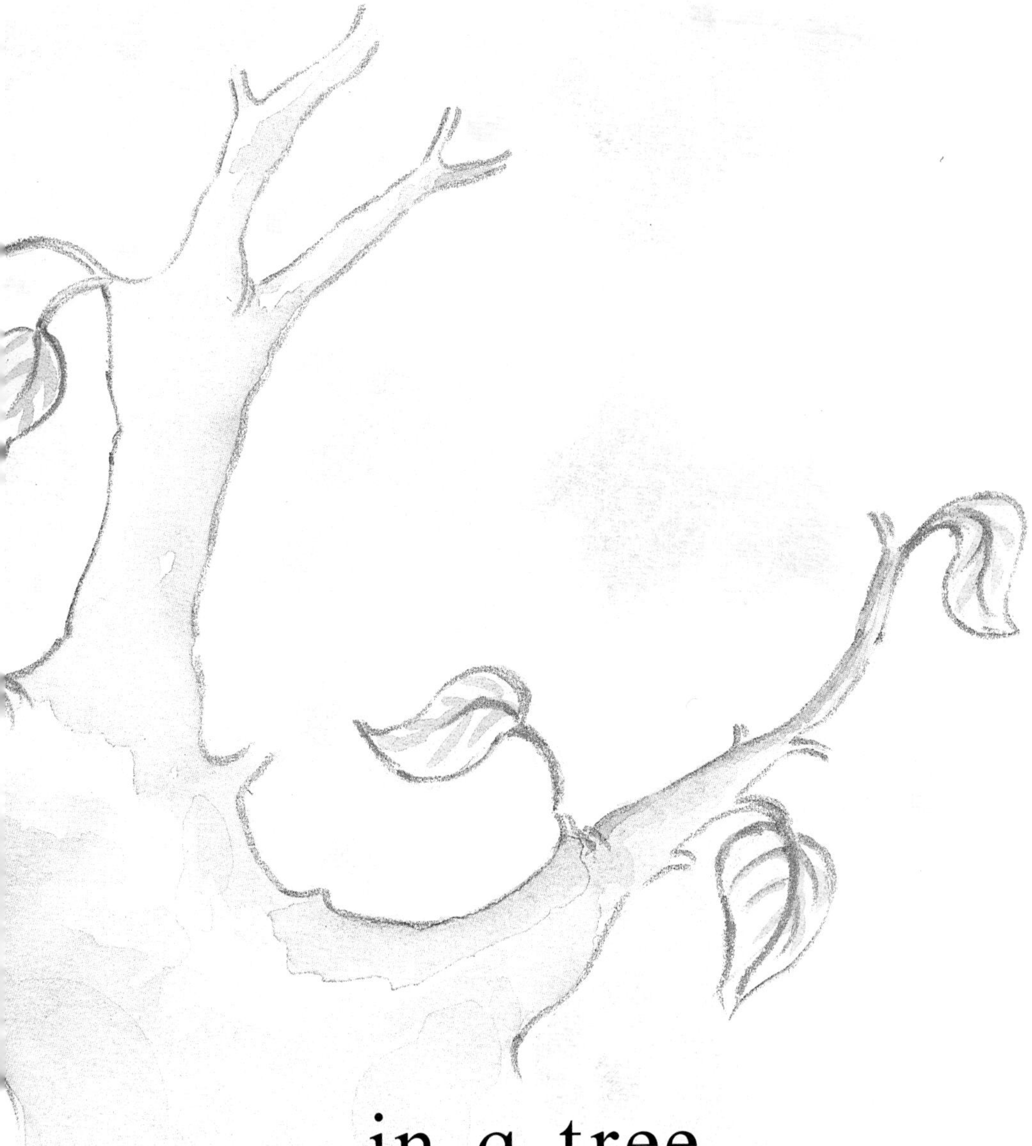

in a tree

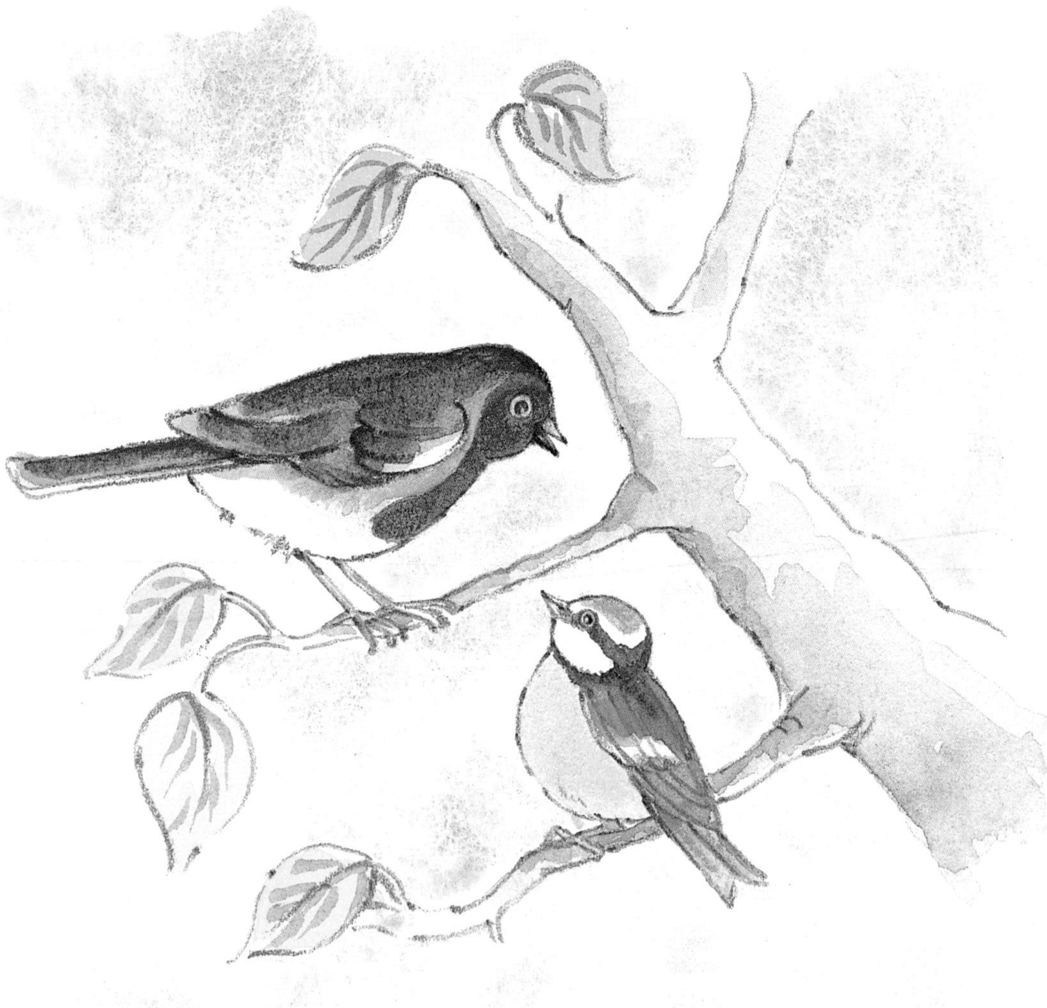

two birds

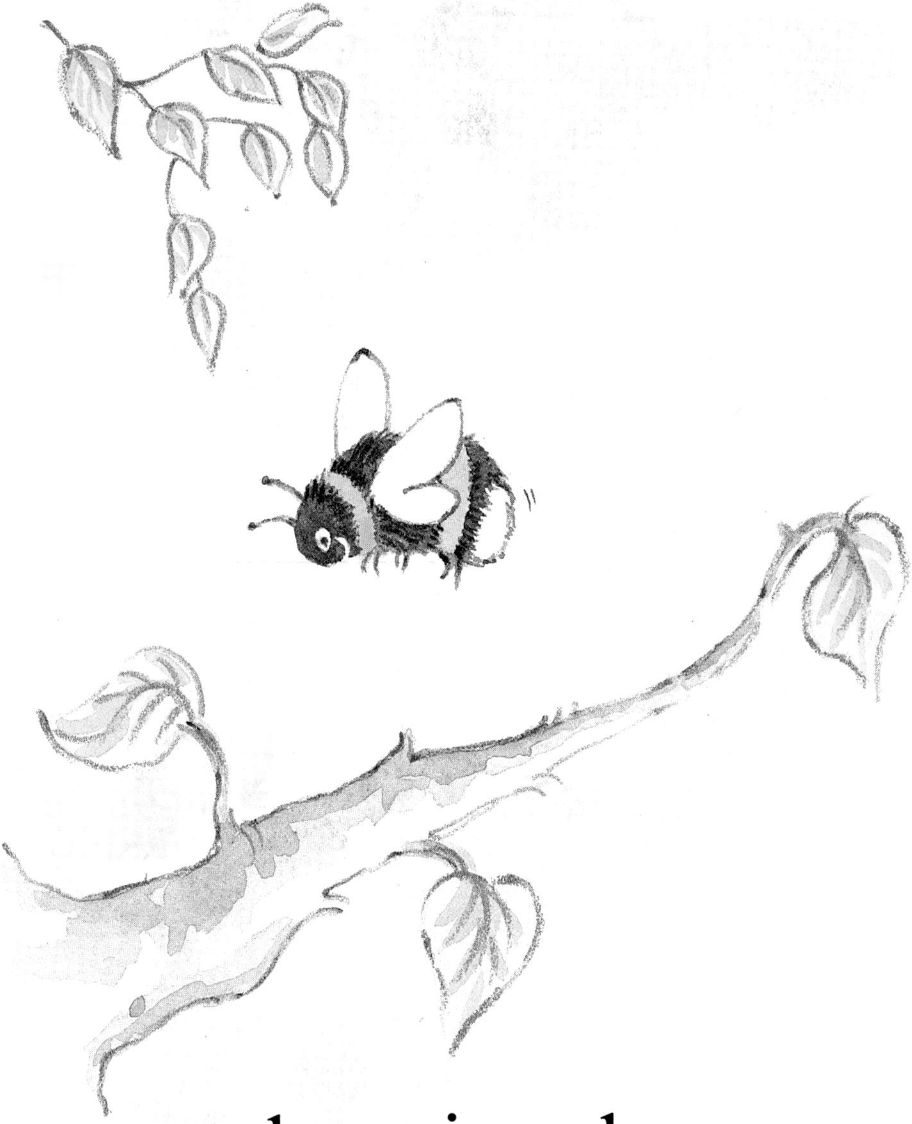

a buzzing bee

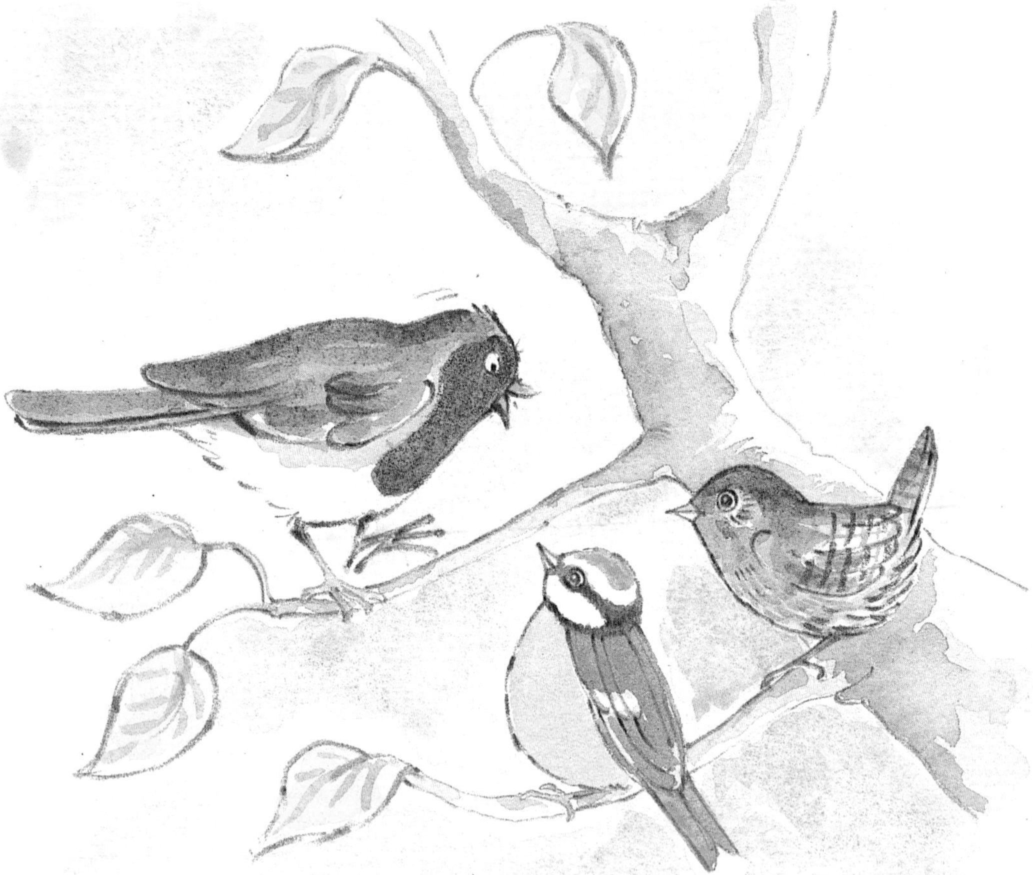

three birds

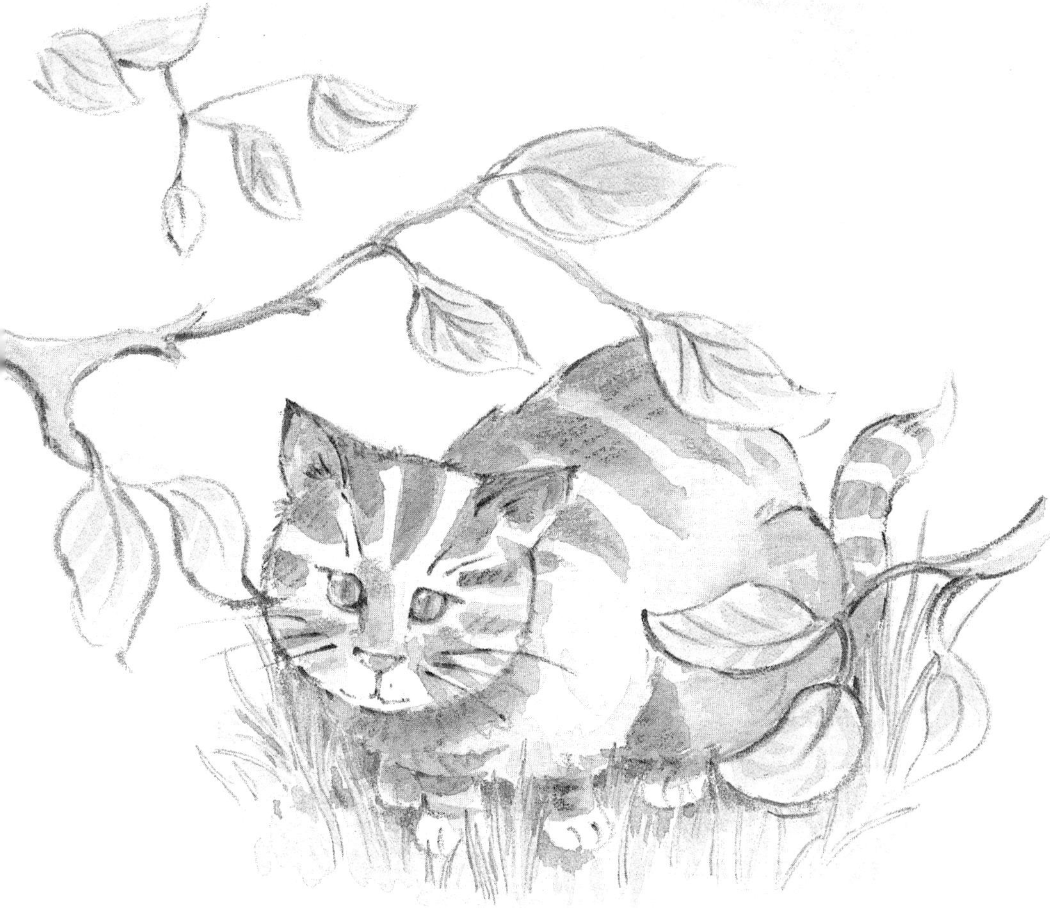

a big fat cat

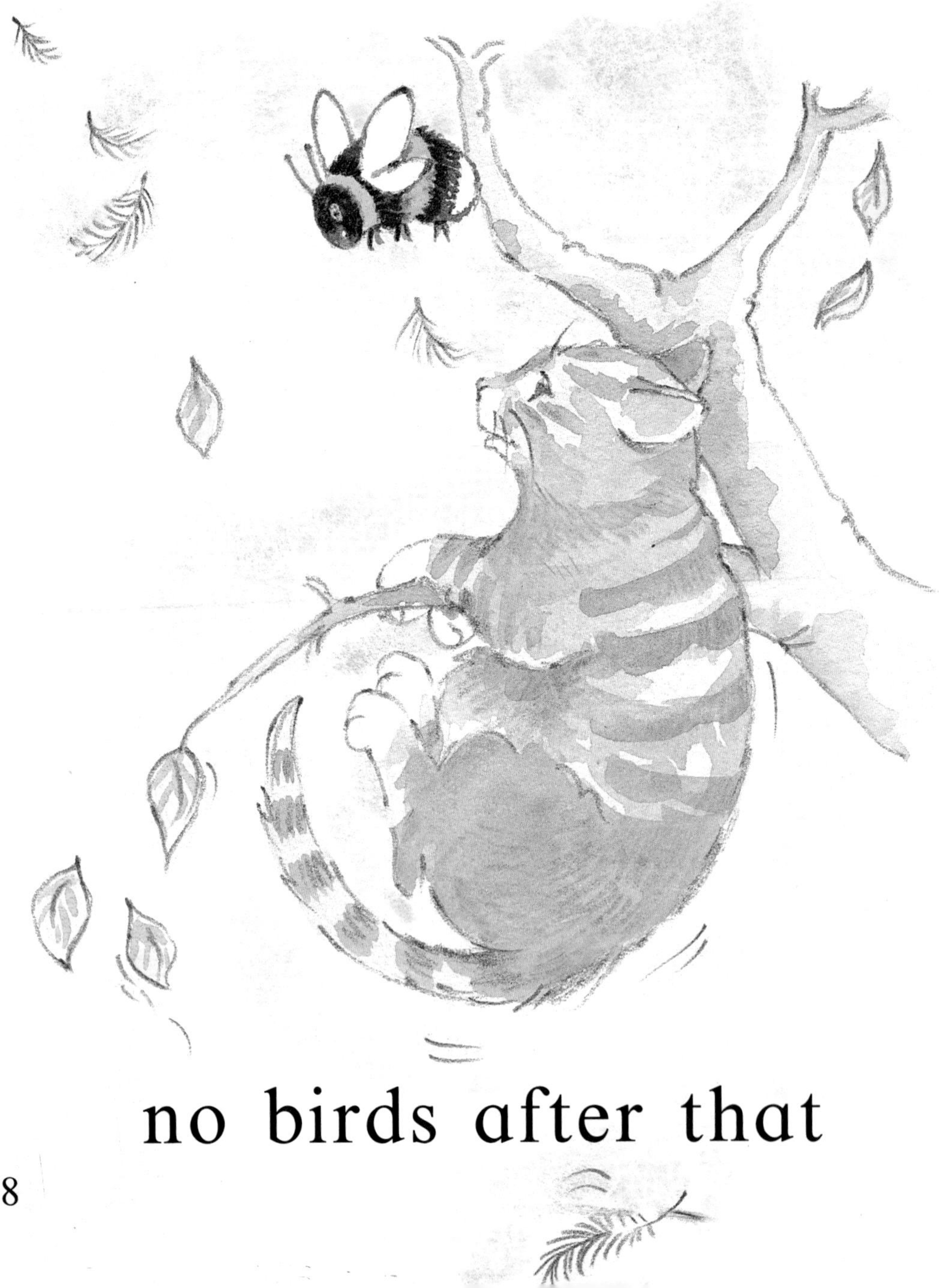

no birds after that